WILLIAM SHATNER

A Little Golden Book® Biography

By Bruce Hale

Illustrated by Martín Morón

🌱 A GOLDEN BOOK • NEW YORK

Text copyright © 2023 by Bruce Hale
Cover art and interior illustrations copyright © 2023 by Martín Morón
All rights reserved. Published in the United States by Golden Books, an imprint of
Random House Children's Books, a division of Penguin Random House LLC, 1745 Broadway,
New York, NY 10019. Golden Books, A Golden Book, A Little Golden Book, the G colophon,
and the distinctive gold spine are registered trademarks of Penguin Random House LLC.
rhcbooks.com
Educators and librarians, for a variety of teaching tools, visit us at RHTeachersLibrarians.com
Library of Congress Control Number: 2022942309
ISBN 978-0-593-56982-5 (trade) — ISBN 978-0-593-56983-2 (ebook)
Printed in the United States of America
10 9 8 7 6 5 4 3 2 1

William Shatner was born on March 22, 1931, in Montreal, Canada. It was the time of the Great Depression, and people throughout Canada and the United States were struggling. Joseph and Anne Shatner worked hard, but they always made sure to have special family time on Sundays with William and his sisters, Farla and Joy.

As a young boy, William liked to play hockey and football in the street with his friends. But above all, he loved watching movies and listening to radio shows. The stories fired his imagination.

Soon William grew interested in performing. He joined the Montreal Children's Theatre, an acting school for kids. He performed in plays and radio dramas. William loved to act—and he never got stage fright!

He wasn't just a theater kid, however. William was on the football and baseball teams in high school, and he enjoyed skiing in the mountains near Montreal.

William went to college at McGill University, where he acted in more plays. William's dad was worried that his son wouldn't be able to make a living as an actor, so he made William promise to get a "practical" degree in commerce. The business skills William learned in college landed him a job as assistant manager for Mountain Playhouse in Montreal after graduation.

Unfortunately, William lost that job when it became clear that he wasn't good with money! He knew he belonged onstage, not behind the scenes, so Mountain Playhouse hired him as an actor instead.

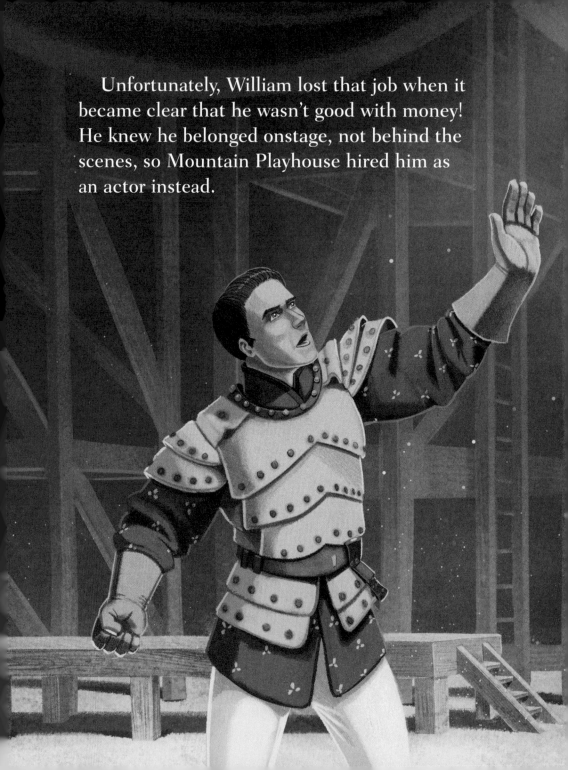

William went on to perform at the Canadian National Repertory Theatre in Ottawa, and then at the Stratford Shakespeare Festival. There he acted in plays, such as *Julius Caesar* and *The Merchant of Venice*, both written by the famous playwright William Shakespeare.

One day, when one of the other actors got sick, William went on in his place with no rehearsal! It had never occurred to him that he might fail. The critics gave him good reviews.

New opportunities began to arrive for William. Television was growing in popularity, and he was cast as Ranger Bob in the Canadian version of the kids' program *The Howdy Doody Show*. In those early days, many TV programs aired live. That meant if you made a mistake, everybody saw it! But William didn't mind. He loved being in front of the camera.

In 1957, William began to act in TV shows in the United States, including an episode of *The Twilight Zone*. Throughout the 1960s, he appeared in dozens of other popular TV series, too, playing lawyers, spies, criminals, and cowboys.

William met Gloria Rand while working on a TV show. Gloria was also an actor. The couple married in 1956. They had three daughters— Leslie, Lisabeth, and Melanie. William was busy juggling family life with his acting career. But things were about to get even busier!

Writer Gene Roddenberry created a show called *Star Trek,* which he described as a Western set in outer space. It featured the voyages of the *Starship Enterprise,* commanded by Captain James T. Kirk. Gene asked William to play Captain Kirk. William took the job—and he was glad he did!

In each episode, Captain Kirk and his crew traveled to new worlds while looking for new civilizations.

Star Trek ran for three years. It wasn't a hit when it aired, but viewers loved its message. Even the U.S. space program, which hadn't yet sent a man to the moon, was inspired by the show's vision of hope and future space travel.

The show may not have lasted long, but William's friendship with the actor who played Mr. Spock certainly did. William and his costar Leonard Nimoy remained close after the show ended.

After *Star Trek* was canceled in 1969, William had trouble finding work because everyone thought of him as Captain Kirk. But William persevered. He played small roles in a wide range of TV shows.

Meanwhile, something unexpected happened. *Star Trek* became more and more popular as people rewatched the old episodes. It was turned into a cartoon series, and then ten years after the original show had been canceled, *Star Trek: The Motion Picture* came to theaters. Viewers loved Captain Kirk and his crew! Six more *Star Trek* movies were made, one of which William directed.

Star Trek fans, known as "Trekkies," or "Trekkers," love to dress up as their favorite characters and attend conventions to discuss the show and meet the actors. William has attended many *Star Trek* conventions over the years. Fans wait in line for hours to see him!

William went on to have many creative projects beyond *Star Trek*. In 2004, he played a lawyer in the final season of *The Practice*. William's character in that TV show was so beloved that he starred in a spinoff series called *Boston Legal*. He won Emmy Awards for playing the role in both shows.

Being a natural storyteller, William has written books, too—books about his life, several novels set in the *Star Trek* universe, and a series of science fiction books called TekWar. He even recorded eight albums—although William speaks the songs instead of singing them!

William has other passions, too. He rides horses for fun and in competitions. He started the Hollywood Charity Horse Show, a yearly event that raises money for children's and veterans' charities.

And William loves being a grandfather! The Sunday family time he has enjoyed since he was a young boy is now spent with his grown daughters and their children.

William has been an actor for over eighty years—on radio, on TV, on the stage, and in movies. His role as Captain Kirk made him famous all over the world!

But maybe his most surprising achievement happened in October 2021. At ninety years old, William became the oldest person to fly into space. Quite a fitting voyage for Captain Kirk!